INMATE ENTREPRENEURIAL PROGRESS

A Guide to Legally Starting a Business,
Investing, Engaging in Real Estate, and
Doing Business via Business Deals
While Incarcerated in the United States

By Travis E. Williams

2015

Inmates for Entrepreneurial Progress

Copyright © 2015 by Travis Eugene Williams.

All rights reserved. Printed in the United States of America. Except as permitted under the Copyright Act of 1976, no part of this publication may be reproduced or distributed in any form or by any means, or stored in a database or retrieval system, with the exception that the program listings may be entered, stored, and executed in a computer system, but they may not be reproduced for publication without the permission of the publisher.

INMATES FOR ENTREPRENEURIAL PROGRESS

A Guide to Legally Starting a Business, Investing, Engaging in Real Estate, and Doing Business via Business Deals While Incarcerated in the United States

By Travis E. Williams

TABLE OF CONTENTS

ACKNOWLEDGMENTS 5
INTRODUCTION 1
CHAPTER 1 THE FOUNDATION 1
CHAPTER 2 THE BASICS OF CONTRACTS AND AGREEMENTS 3
CHAPTER 3 PROPERTY 7
CHAPTER 4 THE ESSENTIALS OF BUSINESS 11
CHAPTER 5 BUSINESS STRUCTURES AND REGISTRATION..18
CHAPTER 6 MISSION STATEMENTS, GOALS AND OBJECTIVES, AND BUSINESS PLANS 25
CHAPTER 7 THE BASICS OF TAXES 31
CHAPTER 8 ORGANIZING YOUR PAPERWORK 35
CHAPTER 9 GETTING THE BALL ROLLING 38
CHAPTER 10 MAKING DEALS 45
CHAPTER 11 INVESTING 49
CHAPTER 12 ENGAGING IN REAL ESTATE 53
APPENDIX A POWER OF ATTORNEY QUESTIONNAIRE 1
APPENDIX B LIMITED POWER OF ATTORNEY..1
APPENDIX C GENERAL POWER OF ATTORNEY 1
APPENDIX D AGENT'S CERTIFICATION AS TO THE VALIDITY OF POWER OF ATTORNEY AND AGENT'S AUTHORITY 1
APPENDIX E SAMPLE TRUST AGREEMENT 1
APPENDIX F (SAMPLE) CERTIFICATE/MEMORANDUM OF TRUST AGREEMENT.......1
APPENDIX G (SAMPLE) APPOINTMENT OF SUCCESSOR TRUSTEE 1
APPENDIX H CONFIDENTIALITY AGREEMENT 1
APPENDIX I OPTION AGREEMENT FOR THE PURCHASE OF REAL PROPERTY 1
APPENDIX J ASSIGNMENT AGREEMENT..1
APPENDIX K NOTICE OF ASSIGNMENT 1
APPENDIX L START-UP STEPS..1
APPENDIX M RESOURCES 1
ABOUT THE AUTHOR..

ACKNOWLEDGMENTS

I would like to offer thanks and sincere gratitude to the many people who played a part in my life's experiences (both good and bad) because without them, maybe I would've never been able to grow into the positive, strong, independent man I am today. Most of all, I want to thank the many people of various backgrounds and lifestyles who continue to stand as perfect examples (both good and bad) which helps guide my better judgment in my pursuit of being a better person. Thank you all. I would like to give a special thanks to Audrey, Moof and Ali, Yvonne, Lavoris, and my beloved Terease.

INTRODUCTION

Inmates for Entrepreneurial Progress is designed to teach and or refresh inmates regarding the need to know basics of starting a business, investing, engaging in real estate, and making business deals while incarcerated in the United States.

Inmates for Entrepreneurial Progress (IEP) is not only a guide, it's a mission and growing movement of incarcerated individuals within the United States who are trying to proactively take their rehabilitation and entrepreneurial aspirations into their own hands, in pursuit of positive change and legal entrepreneurial success while incarcerated (and beyond).

IEP's mission is to show and maintain positive change through productive incarceration by means of self-rehabilitation, pursuing higher education, legally executing entrepreneurial/business plans via agents/fiduciaries on the outside, working to build and or become a part of supportive networks in efforts to continue in personal as well as financial growth, and working hard to be able to provide for their families' despite being incarcerated.

All information is provided in a simple and easy to navigate format, so take your time and use this guide to your benefit. The information contained herein is presented as educational information only and is not to be construed as legal advice. The reader, receiver, and user assume all responsibility and liability. Travis Eugene Williams, author and publisher, assume none. None of the presented information, in any way, applauds or condones criminal activity.

CHAPTER 1,

THE FOUNDATION

CHAPTER 1

THE FOUNDATION

Being incarcerated can be one of the best times to pursue small- to large-scale entrepreneurial endeavors in light of having lots of free time to read, study, plan and develop. In fact, starting a business, investing, engaging in real estate, and/or doing business via business deals is something that a lot of inmates aspire to. It is more than often assumed that being incarcerated prevents inmates from executing their entrepreneurial plans while they are incarcerated, however, that is not the case—inmates can execute their entrepreneurial plans while incarcerated.

So, how do inmates go about executing their entrepreneurial plans while they are incarcerated? The first step for inmates seeking to start a business, invest, engage in real estate, and/or do business via business deals while incarcerated in the United States is to know and understand the following key points:

1. Inmates can legally enter into lawful contractual agreements.

2. Starting a business enterprise (i.e. with a registered business entity) and doing business via business deals (i.e. without a registered business entity) are totally different functions.

3. Existing laws and facility rules within the United States generally prohibit inmates from directly: owning and/or actively participating in business enterprises; investing; and owning real and/or personal property out in the free world.

4. Contracts of agency and trust agreements provide legal routes for inmates to get things done (e.g., start businesses, invest and engage in real estate) in the free world via agents and/or trustees.

Inmates have the right to enter into lawful contractual agreements just as everyone else living out in the free world. This right is called freedom of contract (also called freedom to contract or liberty of contract), as guaranteed under the contract clause of Article I, section 10 of the United States Constitution. However, a grave majority of inmates fail to exercise their right to enter into contractual agreements due to their overall unawareness of such right and/or a lack of resources, proper planning or other. On the other hand, some inmates mildly exercise their right to enter into contractual agreements by doing such things as signing publishing agreements with book publishers, and taking distance learning courses with monthly payment plans—to name a few. Freedom of contract allows incarcerated individuals to lawfully enter into contractual agreements, and thus provides a legal path for inmates to exercise their ability to negotiate contracts, make deals, and potentially turn profits.

Starting a business enterprise and doing business via business deals are totally different functions. Business enterprises consist of fictitious name registration, business entity registration, licensing, and a list of other things that inmates will need an agent and possibly a trustee to take care of. Doing business via business deals simply consists of exercising your right to enter into contractual agreements, reaching out to potential business associates, presenting and proposing ideas, and negotiating deals with hopes and aims to closing the deal. Doing business via business deals can be done by inmates without the need of an agent or trustee, however, deals resulting in the gain of real estate and/or personal property existing out in the free world will require an agent and/or trustee to take charge of the property while the inmate is incarcerated. Some business deals may call for an account to be opened and managed on the outside and this will require an agent and possibly a trustee as well.

In the realm of doing business via business deals, the most common business deal arrangements are: assignment agreements, book sales agreements, consignment agreements, contracts of agency, cross-promotion/co-marketing agreements, co-authorships, distribution agreements, fulfillment service agreements, affiliate program agreements, management service agreements, manufacturing agreements, marketing agreements, sponsorship agreements, endorsement agreements, property management agreements, web design and development agreements, referral agreements, work for hire agreements, partnership agreements, strategic alliance agreements, supplier agreements, and trust agreements—to list a few. Of the many available arrangements, two of the most notable arrangements are contracts of agency and trust agreements. Contracts of agency and trust agreements are excellent legal routes for reaching beyond the walls to execute entrepreneurial plans as an inmate.

To understand how a contract of agency works, let's review the basics of the principal-agent relationship that forms a contract of agency. In a principal-agent relationship (also called agency) the principal is represented by the agent in business or personal affairs with third parties. The principal is the person or business entity that legally authorizes an agent to represent and otherwise act on behalf of the principal. The agent (also called attorney-in-fact) is the person or business entity that legally represents and otherwise acts on behalf of the principal. The overall agreement between the principal and the agent is called a **contract of agency**. The rights and duties of the principal and the agent are usually stated in the contract of agency. Also the term of agency and all other stipulations between the principal and the agent is stated in the contract of agency. A documented contract of agency is called a **power of attorney**. A power of attorney can be general or limited. A general power of attorney gives the agent full authority to act on behalf of the principal. A limited power of attorney gives the agent limited authority to act on behalf of the principal, and is usually to assign specific tasks. When an agent signs documents on behalf of a principal, the agent is to sign the principal's name and then put "by [the agent's name], his (or her) attorney in fact." For example: "_____ (principal's name), by _____ (agent's name), his (or her) attorney-in-fact."

The authority of an agent can be either expressed or implied. Expressed authority specifies instructions in agency agreements orally or in writing. Implied authority is reasonably assumed authority by the agent on behalf of the principal that relates to the express authority given by the principal. For example, implied authority gives the agent authority to make purchases using the principal's credit in cases where purchases are required on behalf of the principal.

In the realm of authority, it is important to understand apparent authority also. When a third party reasonably assumes that an agent has authority beyond the assigned authority granted to the agent, this reasonable assumption is called apparent authority.

An agency is a contractual agreement and can be terminated by fulfillment of duties, by agreement, a dismissal of the agent, or by the prevailing operation of law. However, an agency agreement can be irrevocable (called an irrevocable agency, or an agency coupled with an interest). This happens when an agency contract stipulates that the agent has an interest in the agency (such as salary, commissions, etc.) that the agent receives for his or her services.

Contracts of agency and or a power of attorney should always include a hold harmless and indemnification clause, and an accommodation disclaimer to protect the agent against liability. See the sample power of attorney agreements in the appendixes for examples.

Now that we have reviewed the basics of a contract of agency, let's review some basics regarding ownership to better understand the benefits of trust agreements.

Ownership exists in various and distinctively different forms. In this case let's focus solely on direct ownership and indirect ownership. Direct ownership refers to legal owners of record with legal title. Direct ownership can be held by either an absolute owner or a nominal owner. Absolute ownership is ownership by a single party (i.e., an individual or entity) with the right to exclusive use, and control of the property. Nominal owners have apparent ownership that is not actual. For example, nominal owners usually hold the legal title to the property that someone else is the beneficial owner of. Indirect ownership refers to beneficial owners. Beneficial owners have legal rights to, as well as enjoys the benefits of property that another party (or other parties) is the nominal owner of.

Trust agreements stipulate the terms of trusts established between one or more trustees and one or more beneficiaries. A **trust** is an arrangement where one or more trustees (i.e. individuals or business entities) hold and otherwise manages the property of one or more beneficiaries as the nominal owner for the benefit of the beneficiary or beneficiaries.

Agents and trustees are both fiduciaries. A fiduciary is a person or entity of which property and or power is entrusted for the benefit of another

Contracts of agency and trust agreements are ideal and necessary for inmates to comply with existing laws and rules that prohibit inmates from doing a lot of things directly (i.e., own or actively participate in a business enterprise, etc.).

Existing laws and rules of local, state, and federal facilities within the United States regarding inmates owning and operating businesses, investing, and owning real estate generally states that:

"Incarcerated individuals may not directly own or actively participate in a business, enterprise, and that upon and during the term of their incarceration inmates must assign all of their business affairs, investment affairs, and affairs regarding real estate to the charge of an "agent", committee, or trustee." Note: State laws may vary from state to state, and facility rules may vary from facility to facility. Furthermore, laws and rules are subject to change, so it is wise to keep up with any changes.

Correspondence with business/personal representatives is usually permitted by facilities on a national level to enable inmates to protect personal resources and/or their financial interest.

Now that you understand that exercising your legal right to enter into contractual agreements establishes the foundation to entrepreneurial freedom as an inmate, it is up to you to legally pursue your entrepreneurial goals. Just remember to properly plan.

CHAPTER 2,

THE BASICS OF CONTRACTS AND AGREEMENTS

CHAPTER 2

THE BASICS OF CONTRACTS AND AGREEMENTS

In light of Chapter 1 and its reference to contracts of agency (also called power of attorney), let's review the basics of contracts and agreements.

Contracts are legally enforceable agreements that are created when two or more competent parties agree to perform or avoid performing certain acts of which they have a legal right to do and of which meet legal requirements. All contracts are in fact agreements, however, all agreements are not contracts. This is because agreements often deal with social or personal matters that are not enforceable by law. Agreements are when two or more parties mutually consent to something. An enforceable contract results only when an agreement imposes a legal obligation, but if the agreement only imposes social or moral obligations, its not a contract nor is it legally enforceable.

Contracts are created for many reasons. These reasons may include the sale of particular service(s), product(s), idea(s), employment, licensing for the use of intellectual property, or transfer of title to real or personal property. Contracts may be extended and revised as necessary.

In order for a contract to be legally enforceable, it must contain six elements: Offer and Acceptance, Mutual Consent, Consideration, Competent Parties, Lawful Purpose, and Proper Form. If any of these elements are missing, courts will most likely refuse to enforce the contract.

Offer and acceptance. Offers are proposals made by one or more parties, called offerer(s), to one or more other parties, called offeree(s), that shows a willingness to enter a contract. Acceptance is simply the offeree(s)'s consent to be bound by the terms of the offer.

Mutual consent. All parties to a contract must have a clear understanding regarding what they are undertaking. Thus, a contract must show a meeting of the mind (also referred to as a mutual agreement).

Consideration. Consideration is an exchange of promises. This exchange consists of each party involved in the contract promising either to give up something of value that they have a lawful right to keep, or to do something that they are not legally required to do.

Competent parties. All parties to a contract must be capable of understanding what they are undertaking, that is, be competent. They must also be of normal mentality and legal age. The thinking capacity of a party's mind must not be impaired by the influence of drugs or alcohol, injury, or mental disease.

Lawful purpose. The contract must have lawful purpose (meaning the intent of the actual contract must not, in any way, violate the law). Courts can't enforce contracts that violate the law.

Proper form. Proper form requires contracts that can't be fulfilled in a year, and contracts that involve the sale of property valued at $500 or more to be in writing to be enforceable. Other contracts must be in writing and contain the signatures of all parties. However, it is highly recommended to have all contracts in writing with the signatures of all parties, as well as a witnessing party (such as a notary public, attorney, or other).

These elements constitute a legally enforceable contract. Contracts and agreements alike can be either oral or written, however, written contracts and agreements are more favorable because they provide tangible proof of a contract or agreement.

Contracts and agreements can also be either express or implied. Express contracts and agreements specifically states the agreement of the parties. Implied contracts and agreements do not specifically state the agreement of the parties, however, the terms of the agreement can be inferred from the actions or conduct of the parties, the condition or circumstances, or the customs of the trade. For example: An implied contract or agreement results any time a buyer requests a seller to deliver goods or services to the buyer without mentioning payment. The buyer implies that the goods or services will be paid for at market value upon delivery.

Last but not least, whether a contract is valid, void, or voidable ultimately determines if the contract can be enforced. Valid contracts are agreements that establish obligations that are legally enforceable. Void contracts are agreements that lack one or more of the six elements that makes a contract legally enforceable. Voidable contracts are agreements that can be rejected by one of the parties of the agreement for a lawful and acceptable reason.

CHAPTER 3,

PROPERTY

CHAPTER 3

PROPERTY

In Chapter 1 we discussed direct and indirect ownership, in this chapter we will discuss property. Property is defined as something that is owned or possessed. There are three main types of property. These three main types of property are personal property, real property, and intellectual property.

Personal property is property (such as vehicles, clothing, etc.) that is movable. Real property (also called real estate) is property (such as land, buildings, structures, crops, and other resources that are attached to or within the land) that is immovable. Intellectual property is intangible property that is the end result of creativity. It can be expressions of ideas, knowledge, and methods of doing things.

To safeguard intellectual property, protection such as copyrights, patents, trade secrets, trademarks, and service marks are available.

Copyrights are granted protection from the government to creators of artistic, creative, or literary works (i.e. music, magazines, books, videos, maps, motion pictures, etc.). Copyrighted material is usually noted by the © symbol. When copyrighted materials are copied without permission, this is called infringement. However, the "fair use" doctrine usually allows limited copying (i.e., to be used for news reporting, research, parody, criticism, or education).

Patents are granted protection from the government to inventors. Patents give the inventor(s) the exclusive right to use, manufacture, and/or sell the invention. The term for patent protection is usually 20 years. Any selling or manufacturing of patented product without permission is also infringement. Also, design patents are available to both business firms and individuals to protect unique figures, shapes, and patterns (such as soft-drink bottles, etc.). The term for design patents is 20 years also.

Trade secrets are specialized practices, devices, manufacturing processes, and confidential information regarding a particular business that could give business competition a serious advantage. Protecting trade secrets generally consists of confidentiality agreements and imposing restrictions. These restrictions usually exist in the form of "restrictive covenants," and "agreements not to compete." Restrictive covenants are agreements where employees agree not to work for similar businesses. Agreements not to compete are agreements where the seller(s) of said trade secrets agree not to start or otherwise operate a similar business. This agreement not to compete can be (1) for a specified geographic area, (2) a specified duration, or (3) both.

Trademarks and servicemarks. A trademark is any symbol, name, word, or design used by either a merchant or manufacturer to distinguish his or her products from products manufactured by others. Trademarks can also exist as a combination of any symbol, name, word, or design. Trademarks allow consumers to know who particular products are manufactured by for choice of preference. Trademarks are usually displayed in advertisings, letterheads, labels, and packaging, with the word "registered," the symbol ™, or the symbol ®. A service mark is similar to a trademark, however, a service mark identifies a source of service. The service mark symbol is "SM" the word "registered," or the symbol ®. Trademarks and service marks exist to prevent others from profiting off of your trademarks and/or service marks without permission.

Trade dress is a very useful tool in the realm of trademarks and service marks. Trade dress is a nonfunctional, but unique feature that distinguishes a given manufacturer or merchant and the goods or services of a given manufacturer or merchant from other manufacturers and merchants. These unique features include the total image, color coordination, etc.

Obtaining permission (also called licensing) to use, manufacture, and/or sell someone else's copyrighted material, patented inventions and/or designs, trade secrets, and trademarks or service marks generally consists of making a request to do so to the copyright, patent, trade secret, trademark or service mark holder(s). Before permission is granted, the terms of use, manufacturing, sell and other must be arranged and agreed upon. This agreement is usually in the form of permission and/or a licensing agreement. Cross-permission/cross-licensing allows mutual use of each other's intellectual property.

CHAPTER 4,

THE ESSENTIALS OF BUSINESS

CHAPTER 4

THE ESSENTIALS OF BUSINESS

In order to do business and be effective in doing it, you need to know the essentials of business. Here the essentials of business are divided into two categories: the basic elements of business, and basic business obligations.

The basic elements of business consist of products and services, money and finance, research and development, location, contracts and agreements, marketing, sales, bookkeeping, accounting, and management.

Products and Services. The concept of business revolves around offering a product or service for monetary gains. Products and services exist in many different forms.

Money and Finance. Money is a medium used for exchange, usually in the form of currency (i.e., cash and coins). Finance is the management of money. Finances is monetary resources. Financing is to supply another with money (or credit) or to be supplied with money (or credit). The primary forms of financing are cash loans and credit. A loan is when a sum of money is borrowed from a lender under the conditions that the loan will be repaid, usually with interest. With loans, the borrower is known as the loanee, and the lender is known as the loaner. Credit is the granted ability to obtain goods or services before payment based on the trust that payment for the goods or services will be made in the future. Credit can be revolving. Revolving credit is credit that may be used recurrently up to the limit specified after partial or total repayments are made. With credit, the debtor is who receives credit, and the creditor is who grants credit. Both loans and credit can be issued with or without interest obligations. Loans and credit can be repaid in either installments or lump sums depending on the terms of agreement. Installments are principal payments of the principal (and usually interest) divided into several payments to be paid over a period of time. Lump sums are single payments of a principal all at one time (usually with all interest) as opposed to installments. The principal is the total of the sum or value of the thing(s) lent in a loan or credit. Interest is money paid for the use of money (or things) lent, or for delaying the repayment of a debt. Interest is usually charge by rate and the interest rate is a percentage of the principal. Interest can be simple or compound. Simple interest is interest that applies to the principal only, for the entire duration of the transaction. Compound interest is interest that builds on itself. Unlike simple interest, compound interest allows interest gains to be added with the principal (i.e., monthly, quarterly, or annually) so that interest can be earned not only on the principal but on all previously earned interest as well.

Research and Development (also called R&D). Research and development generally refers to the labor directed towards the overall innovation in and the improvements of a company's products, services, and/or ideas. Research is an investigation into and study of materials and sources in order to discover or verify information. Research is vital because it allows you to generate information that can ultimately determine whether your business venture(s) will fail or be a success. In the field of business, research is usually used to:

- Identify a need and a niche in the marketplace
- Identify current and future markets
- Determine how to generate profit
- Identify consumer trends
- Identify the local market(s)
- Identify national and international markets
- Gain and keep abreast of industry knowledge
- Identify inexpensive manufacturing and production methods
- Establish operational cost projections
- Identify proper licensing, registration, and permit requirements for the particular business venture(s)
- Identify the best marketing and sales methods
- Identify and keep abreast of federal, state, and local laws and regulations that effect the particular business operations
- Identify possible unforeseen losses, set-backs, and liability expenses
- And consider information in general to determine its significance regarding business success.

Research provides a means for proper preparation, and therefore should be used to its fullest extent. Development is bringing, growing, or evolving someone or something to a more complete and advanced state.

Location. Location is a particular place and represents the particular place(s) that a business does or will be doing business in. This refers both to online and traditional brick and mortar set-ups.

Contracts and Agreements. The basics of contracts and agreements are discussed in Chapter 2.

Marketing. Marketing is the process of creating, pricing, promoting, and distributing goods, services, and ideas to potential customers in an effort to establish and maintain exchange relationships with customers and potential customers. The creation of goods, services, and ideas usually starts with one or more creative minds, and identifying a niche and need in a particular market. Although there are many different pricing methods, the pricing of goods, services, and ideas generally consist of adding a dollar amount or percentage to the cost of the overall production of the goods, services, and ideas to set a price base for wholesale or retail. The production of goods, services, and ideas usually bring forth expenses for research and development, manufacturing the product(s), and general labor for service(s) provided. The two major factors for pricing are supply and demand, and competitive pricing. Supply and demand is the amount of a particular good or service available (i.e., supply) versus the desire of customers for it (i.e., demand), considered as overall factors regulating the price for the particular good(s) or service(s). Competitive pricing is pricing that is influenced primarily by the competitor's prices. Promotion is the publicizing of a product, service, or idea to increase sales and/or public awareness of the particular product, service, or idea. Promotion consists of using multiple methods to present your product(s), service(s), or idea(s) to potential customers. These methods usually consist of networking, displaying at trade shows, contacting the media with press releases, advertising (via newspapers, tv, radio, internet, magazines, etc.), offering coupon discounts, giving flyers and handouts, brochures, requesting and offering referrals, and e-mail campaigns— to list a few. Distribution is simply supplying goods to a number of recipients, especially retailers.

Effective marketing begins with a plan. This plan is called a marketing plan. Marketing plans can be simple or complex, and usually consist of detailed information regarding your ideas and timelines for marketing your product(s), service(s), or idea(s). This information may include, yet is not limited to the following: a clear definition of the product(s), service(s), or idea(s) you are selling; a clearly defined target market and an ideal customer profile; a clearly defined competitive edge (i.e., your unique selling proposition— also called USP); price setting; knowledge of where your product(s), service(s), or idea(s) may be positioned in the minds of the customers; clearly defining the best ways to brand your business as well as develop a lasting image; clearly defined promotional strategies; a marketing budget; and a well-prepared sales pitch— to list a few. Proper marketing breeds branding. Branding is a combination of your company's name, logo, slogan, mission statement, and company's theme associated with the company's product(s), service(s), or idea(s) in the eyes and minds of consumers. Branding lets consumers know who you are and what you provide.

Sales. Sales is the profession or activity of selling (i.e., the exchange of goods, services, or ideas for money). Unless a seller and a buyer give mutual consent of exchange, there is no exchange and a sale has not occurred.

In the realm of sales, it is important to understand the basics of warranties. A warranty is a promise or guarantee made by the seller (or manufacturer) that the product(s) or service(s) offered are what they claimed to be or what a reasonable person has a right to expect. Warranties can be express or implied, and full or limited. An express warranty is a guarantee that is suggested or inferred from known facts and circumstances. A full warranty is a promise that defective product(s) will be repaired or replaced with no charge within a reasonable time after a complaint is made. A limited warranty is a warranty that doesn't meet the least requirements of a full warranty.

Bookkeeping. Bookkeeping is the activity of recording financial affairs. Financial affairs are recorded in either a ledger (also called general ledger), subledger, or journal. Ledgers, subledgers, and journals are books and computer memory software programs for posting monetary transactions. These monetary transactions cover every activity from office supply purchases to product or service sales. Each activity has an account where that particular activity is recorded. Each account has a three or more digit number (usually four) that makes it easy to locate particular accounts in a ledger, subledger, or journal. These individual accounts are then compiled to form a chart of accounts. A chart of accounts is an organized list that classifies a company's usual sources of revenue and expenses and usually mirrors sections on financial statements. General ledgers contain a record of all financial affairs combined, whereas subledgers and journals usually contain a record of particular accounts. The process of entering financial transactions into either a general ledger, subledger, or journal is called posting. Posting includes giving a brief summary of the transaction(s) with a reference number to any source documents. Source documents generally consist of receipts, invoices, bills, etc. Transactions posted into a general ledger, subledger, or journal (such as loans, loan drawdowns, sales, asset acquisitions, asset sales, investor capital contributions, etc.) are called journal entries. A simple entry will include the date of the transaction, a brief description of the transaction, the total amount of money involved in the transaction, and a reference to any source document(s). Entry descriptions are usually shifted slightly to either the left or the right in a ledger, subledger, or journal to reflect a credit or debit entry, and the total sum involved in the entry is listed in a separate designated column to the right-hand side. However, bookkeeping entry practices may vary depending on how individual bookkeepers choose to keep their books. Every transaction that happens per day must be posted for that day. Batching (also called batch processing) is the recording of multiple similar transactions simultaneously as a time salver. There are generally two entry systems, These two entry systems are single entry and double (or dual) entry. Single entry is a system of bookkeeping where each transaction is entered into one account only. Double (or dual) entry is a system of bookkeeping where each transaction is entered twice, once as a debit in one account and the other as a credit in another account.

Debits and credits are the two kinds of activity that affect financial accounts (i.e., assets, liabilities, equity, revenue, and expense).

Bookkeeping can be either accrual or cash based. Accrual bookkeeping records transactions when they occur regardless of if any money changes hands. Cash based bookkeeping records transactions only when money changes hands.

All records should reflect all yearly transactions on a day-to-day basis in a simple and accurate manner for accounting purposes.

Accounting. There are multiple forms of accounting, but the primary form of accounting is basic accounting. Basic accounting is the process of inspecting financial records. Accountants use the information gathered by bookkeepers in conceptual ways to prepare necessary reports (such as balance sheets, income statements, and cash flow statements) based on that information in efforts to reach a conclusion regarding financial status. Accountants use a simple formula to determine financial status. To determine financial status, liabilities are subtracted from assets and the remainder is its status (also called worth). The balance sheet must always balance out with assets being equal to the sum of liabilities and equity. This happens as a result of accurate entries of debits and credits to asset, liability, equity, expense, and revenue accounts. The income statement reflects profitability, however, it does not tell everything about the financial health of a company (or person). The cash flow statement tracks the flow of cash through a particular business or venture over a period of time. The cash flow statement shows the cash on hand at the beginning of the period, cash received during the period, cash spent during the period, and the cash on hand when the period ends.

Note: It is an IRS auditing requirement that invoices are numbered and a numerical copy maintained in accounting records.

Management. Management is the process of managing commercial and industrial business organizations. Management usually consists of regulating and maintaining the operation of a business venture. For the purpose of effective management, business owners create operation procedures to regulate how their business is to operate. Operational procedures (also called policies) are a set of rules and regulations regarding the operation of a business. These rules and regulations generally govern every facet of business functions (i.e., marketing, sales, customer service, inventory management, employment, asset management, etc.). Customized operating procedures are procedures that are tailored to fit your particular business. If drafting your own operating procedures for your business seems a bit daunting, then perhaps standardized is the route for you. Even better, you can make adjustments to standardized operating procedures to fit your style of operations.

The basic business obligations are generally adhering to the federal and state laws (i.e., the Uniform Commercial Codes, tax laws, labor laws, etc.). and local regulations (such as license and permit requirements) that govern the operation of that particular business.

The Small Business Administration and the Small Business Development Center near you can assist you with references to federal, state, and local regulations that govern the operation of your business. At your discretion, you can have this information researched via prisoner concierge services.

CHAPTER 5,

BUSINESS STRUCTURES AND REGISTRATION

CHAPTER 5

BUSINESS STRUCTURES AND REGISTRATION

There are several different types of business structures. These business structures are sole proprietorships, general partnerships, limited partnerships, limited liability companies, corporations, and business trusts.

Sole proprietorships. A sole proprietorship is an unincorporated business that is owned and operated by one person. This structure is easy to create and very flexible. This structure allows entitlement to all profits with respects to taxes, however, it also renders you (as the owner) personally liable for all business obligations and claims against that business (i.e., your sole proprietorship). Sole proprietorships are taxed at the individual's personal income tax rate.

General partnerships (also called partnerships). A partnership is a business that is owned and operated by two or more people or entities. The shares of the partners may vary according to the agreement between the partners. Generally, the partners agree to share the responsibility for managing the business affairs, the business profits, and the liabilities. In the event of dissolution, the partnership contract should cover death or disability of one or more partners, expulsion of one or more partners, retirement of one or more partners, bankruptcy of the business, and the liquidation of partnership assets— to list a few. Partnerships are fairly easy to create. In regards to partnership liability, "joint and several liability" allows anyone making a claim against the partnership to elect to sue either all the partners or any individual partner(s).

Limited partnerships. A limited partnership is a partnership formed by two or more people or entities and having at least one or more general partner(s) and one or more limited spartner(s). The general partners retain control over the management of they limited partnership and usually are liable for all obligations of the limited partnership. The limited partners usually invest money or property in the business and are entitled to a share of the profits and losses. The limited partners' liability is usually limited to their investment in the business.

Limited liability companies. A limited liability company (also called LLC) is an unincorporated association with usually one or more members. It stands as a separate legal entity and limits the personal liability of all its owners. The owners can act as the management team or elect to hire a management team and share control of the business. With LLCs it is essential to create a LLC operating agreement, i.e. a member-managed agreement or a manager-managed agreement. In a LLC operating agreement, the rules for ownership and operation of the business are set— similar to partnership agreements and corporate bylaws. A basic operating agreement covers the members' share percentage in the business, the rights and responsibilities of the members, the voting power of members, the allocation of profits and losses, management of the LLC, rules regarding meeting and voting, and "buy-sell" provisions. Limited liability company protection also extends to professional services listed under the professional corporation category. This form of LLC is called a professional limited liability company. Limited liability companies are allowed to be taxed as a corporation or a partnership.

Corporations. A corporation is a business entity with a legal existence separate from its owners. Corporations have similar legal rights and privileges as people, such as those granted by the constitution. Corporations also bear their own liability, and thus, shields the corporate owner(s) and officers from negligence on behalf of the corporation. This protective shield is called the corporate veil. In the event of negligence on behalf of the corporate owner(s) and/or officers, claims of "alter ego" can be used in a court of law to hold the controlling members of a corporation personally liable.

There are three different types of corporations. These three types of corporations are non-stock corporations, stock corporations, and professional corporations.

Non-stock corporations (also called private corporations) are not authorized to issue shares of stock, and can be owned by one or more people or entities privately. Non-stock corporations do not have to file financial reports with the securities exchange commission because the are private corporations, and therefore can operate freely in accordance with the general laws governing their business operations (especially the regular payment of taxes and adhering to labor laws and general rules and regulations of uniform commercial codes).

Stock corporations (also called public corporations) are authorized to issue bonds and shares of stock, and thus, are publically owned by the corporations' stock owners (also called stock holders). Bonds are certificates of debt issued promising to repay borrowed money with interest at a specified time. Stocks are tradable securities that indicate ownership in a corporation, usually divided into shares and used to raise capital for the corporation through issuing shares. Shares are equal portions of the capital contributed to a corporation by a number of people (and/or entities) and represents ownership according to the volume of shares individual stock owners own in that corporation. Corporations are allowed to issue either a single class of stock or multiple classes of stock with each class of stock having different rights and privileges. These classes of stock are common stock and preferred stock. Common stock gives the stock holder voting rights, but in the event of corporate liquidation, common stock holders receive claims to corporate assets after preferred stock holders. Preferred stock gives the stockholder priority to receive claims to corporate assets in the event of corporate liquidation, however, preferred stock holders usually don't have voting rights.

Each share of stock is assigned a dollar amount by the corporation. This dollar amount is called the par value. The par value of shares differs from the market value of shares. This is because the market value of shares fluctuates according to the market and overall conditions of the economy. The par value also aids in keeping track of stock splits. Stock splits are divisions of a corporations outstanding shares into a larger number of shares— often to reduce the price per share in efforts to make stocks more desirable to and/or affordable for potential investors. Reverse stock splits are when corporations call in their outstanding shares and reissue fewer shares at higher prices. Shares can also be issued by a corporation with no par. No par stock (also called no par value stock) is stock issued with no par value by a corporation primarily for corporate accounting purposes or other as allowed by law.

Stock corporations come in two forms. These two forms are "C" corporations, and subchapter "S" corporations. A "C" corporation is a business that has received a charter legally recognizing it as a corporation with its own rights, privileges, and liabilities separate from its owners. "C" corporations suffer double taxation. They are taxed once at the corporate level, and taxed again at the individual level. A subchapter "S" corporation is a special status granted by the internal revenue code that permits a corporation to be taxed at the individual rate or sole proprietorship so that profits can be taxed at the individual rate instead of the corporate rate. However, the subchapter "S" corporation status is only available to corporations with fewer than 100 shareholders.

Stock corporations are required by law to pay dividends to stock owners. Dividend payments are usually quarterly. Stock corporations must file public financial reports with the securities exchange commission (SEC). The State Corporation Commission usually mails an annual assessment packet that contains a preprinted annual report form, and a notice of annual registration fee assessment, to the registered agent(s) of the corporation approximately 75 days before the due date for annual reports and registration fee payment.

Note: Stock corporations usually hire investment bankers to assist them through the process of going public (i.e., issuing shares of stock). This includes developing the corporations' prospectus to provide important information to the corporations' potential investors about the corporation.

Professional corporations are authorized to do business as a stock (publically owned) or non-stock (privately owned) corporation. Professional corporations usually consist of one or more people authorized to perform professional services in corporate form. The professional services are usually limited to the personal services rendered by, but not limited to, physical therapists, physical therapist assistants, pharmacists, dentists, surgeons, optometrists, practitioners of the healing arts, nurse practitioners, architects, professional engineers, public accountants, land surveyors, certified public accountants, and attorneys-at-law— to name a few.

The formation of corporations usually requires corporations to draft articles of incorporation, and bylaws. The articles of incorporation is a document that lists the powers of a corporation. The bylaws are rules and regulations controlling the actions of a company's members. A corporate seal is a requirement of some states upon corporations, and all contracts and other legal documents of the corporation must bear the stamp of the corporate seal.

The State Corporation Statute for each individual state will stipulate the management positions (i.e., a board of directors, a CEO or president, a secretary, a treasurer, etc.) that must be filed by each corporation formed in those particular states. In non-stock corporations and small corporations, most states allow one person to fill all the management positions. This is called wearing many corporate hats.

Business trust. A business trust is an unincorporated business, association or trust that is governed by a formal or legal document that outlines the stipulations regarding the property and/or activities of the business trust that is or will be owned, managed, or carried on by one or more trustee(s) for the benefit of one or more beneficial owner(s). A business trust is a separate legal entity and the beneficial owners are usually entitled to the same limited personal liability as the shareholders of stock corporations. Also, the filing of an "articles of trust" is usually required by individual state corporation commissions.

In the realm of business structures, it's important to understand the basics of non-profit organizations and franchising. Businesses that are formed and exist primarily to benefit society are classified as non-profit organizations (also called not-for-profit organizations). Non-profit organizations are usually granted tax exemptions by the IRS. The IRS allows several different exemption statuses, and usually, only non-stock corporations and limited liability companies can be granted a tax exempt status, so be sure to contact the IRS regarding the optional exemption statuses and the business structures that qualify for tax exemption. Non-profit organizations can receive tax-deductible cash and in-kind donations from donors. A franchise is an authorization, usually by a business, granted to one or more people or entities, that allows them to operate one or more businesses bearing the brand of the business granting the franchise while selling the products and/or services associated with that business. The franchiser is the person or entity granting the franchise, and the franchisee is the person or entity that has been granted the franchise. Under a franchise agreement, franchisees are required to pay for the right to market the product(s) and/or service(s) under the franchiser's brand name. This fee also usually covers training and advertising provided by the franchiser. Franchise agreements place restrictions on the franchisee and usually specify the initial investment required to operate the franchise, training the franchiser will provide, geographical territory assigned to the franchisee, brand name and trademark (or service mark) agreements, ongoing royalties and advertising fees paid to the franchiser, operational guidelines, renewal and cancellation terms, and resale agreements. Although franchises give the benefit of selling brand name product(s) and/or service(s), franchisees must answer to the franchiser. Also if ever the brand name of the franchise is tarnished by the negligence of the franchiser or other franchises, it can have a negative effect on your stake in the franchise.

Federal law requires franchisers to provide potential franchisees a copy of the Uniform Franchising Offering Circular (UFOC) prior to offering to sell a franchise. The UFOC is documentation that includes pertinent information regarding the franchiser, and the franchise at hand. The UFOC will include the actual franchise agreement. The franchise agreement for any particular franchise stands as the legal basis of the franchiser-franchisee relationship.

Registration. Business registration is a formal process that is relatively simple and easy.

Step one. Determine what business structure you want to operate under.

Step two. Contact the State Corporation Commission or Corporation Commission for the state(s) your business will be registered in to obtain the proper registration forms and pricing for registration. Registration forms have (and usually come with) instructions for filing, so be sure to obtain the registration instructions for filing with the particular registration forms.

Step three. Complete the registration form(s) and file them with the State Corporation Commission along with full payment of the required registration fees.

Before registering your business structure, you may need to decide whether or not you will be using an assumed or fictitious name to do business as, and if it will be in your best interest to obtain the proper trademarks and/or service marks to protect your assumed or fictitious name.

Domestic v. Foreign. Domestic refers to businesses formed and existing within the state you live in. Foreign refers to businesses formed and existing in a state other than the one you live in.

CHAPTER 6,

**MISSION STATEMENTS, GOALS AND
OBJECTIVES, AND BUSINESS PLANS**

CHAPTER 6

MISSION STATEMENTS, GOALS AND OBJECTIVES, AND BUSINESS PLANS

In this chapter we will review the basics of mission statements, goals and objectives, and business plans.

Mission Statements. A mission statement is one or more paragraphs that briefly and clearly states what you do, where you do it, whom you do it for, and the way you do it or will be doing it— that makes your business different from your competitors. The mission statement is your unique selling proposition (USP) and is very important. Figure 6.1 gives an example of a mission statement.

Figure 6.1

Mission Statement

"Our mission is to promote individual growth on a national level for the incarcerated collectively through business education, supportive networking, and resource awareness, while contributing to the volume of rehabilitation, productive citizenship, and anti-recidivism."

Goals and Objectives. Goals and objectives, although similar, are not the same, but work hand in hand together. The goal is a brief statement of your overall target outcome. Figure 6.2 gives an example of a goal.

Figure 6.2

Goal

"Our goal is to reduce the national recidivism rate."

The objectives are generally a series of statements that fill in the specific details of how your goal(s) will be accomplished. Figure 6.3 gives an example of objectives.

Figure 6.3

Objectives

"Our objectives are (1) to educate incarcerated individuals on how to start and effectively manage a

business or businesses on a national level, and (2) to show them how to locate and utilize available resources in efforts to promote positive productive mind states among inmates to gradually reduce the national recidivism rate while increasing our nation's citizenship rate."

Business Plans. A business plan is generally a written description of a business's future that describes (in full or in partial detail) what that business plans to do and how that business plans to do it. Business plans can vary in length depending on the simplicity of complexity of the plans. A simple business plan can be anywhere from 15 to 20 pages, but a more complex business plan can run up to 100 pages or more. Business plans generally follow common guidelines regarding their form and their content, and usually consist of a cover sheet, a table of contents, and executive summary, a general company description, a product/service section, a marketing strategies section, a operations and management section, a financial section, and an appendix section.

The cover sheet is usually for appealing to investors, and should be kept as simple as possible. The cover sheet should identify you, your business, the date (of presentation), and the prospective investor(s) that you are addressing the business plan to.

The table of contents is an organized index of the business plans content, and helps the reader(s) of your plan navigate their way through your plan.

The executive summary section summarizes the entire business plan at a glance, as an introduction, and is usually one or more pages long. The executive summary should be designed to get and keep the reader's interest, and should be prepared after all other sections to the business plan are complete. The executive summary should include your mission statement, your financial future projections (i.e., for sales, costs, and profits), your operational needs, the requested funding, and your repayment plan— to list a few.

The general company description is an introduction to the business and outlines all the pertinent information about the business. The general company description consists of subsections that outline the general business overview, the company structure, the company's location(s), the company's mission, the company's key management and general labor personnel, the company's goals and objectives, and the company's strengths and weaknesses. The general business overview basically describes the business, where it stand in the marketplace, and the needs it will or is filling. The company structure basically describes the environment in which the business is or will be located in, and its overall accessibility to customers. The company's mission reflects the company's mission statement. The company's key management and general labor personnel subsection show duties and experience of the listed personnel. The goals and objectives subsection should reflect the company's goals and objectives. The strengths and weaknesses subsection should highlight the company's strengths while outlining the company's weaknesses and development strategies to strengthen the company's weaknesses.

The product/service section tells about the product(s) or service(s) you are or tend to be selling. It should provide (1) a full description of the product(s) or service(s), the benefits of your product(s) or service(s), and the need of your product(s) or service(s) in the marketplace, (2) your cost of production or general labor, and (3) any legal ramifications regarding your product(s) or service(s).

The marketing strategies section covers general market research, the competition, and the marketing and sales strategies. General market research basically shows a current market analysis, an outlook of the industry, identifies the target market and the size of the market, identifies the ideal customer profile, and gives other relevant information relating to the marketplace. The competition shows pertinent information regarding the current competition, the competition's strengths and weaknesses, and your advantage over the competition. The marketing and sales strategies generally reflects your marketing plan.

The operation and management section outlines how you will operate your business. It covers your overhead costs, quality control policies regarding relevant hazards or environmental risks with safety procedures that are relevant to your business operation, insurance policies (i.e., a list of insurance policies you have or plan to take out regarding liability, workers compensation, theft and fire, business interruption, key management and employee, etc.), equipment on hand and/or equipment needed with the cost or value and life expectancy per item, licenses and permits required to operate your business (including their cost) that you have obtained or need to obtain, staff positions (including job descriptions, responsibilities, and wages/salaries), any suppliers (including any notable supplier credit stipulations), and the overall distribution of your company's products, services, and/or ideas.

The financial section outlines statements of any past and current business income, expenses, and cash flow with projections of future income, expenses, cash flow, and any additional needed funding. The projections of income and expenses are monthly estimations of revenue and expenses. The first year is usually projected in months, and the following two to five years by quarter, semiannually, or annually. Always be realistic and as accurate as possible when preparing financial projections. The cash flow forecast is different from the revenue and expense projections because it generally estimates when revenues and expenses will be received and paid out. The needed funding portion of the financial section generally outlines how much money is needed, when the money is needed, the specific type of loan or credit that you're applying for, a detailed description of how the funds will be used, and a detailed description of the terms for repayment.

The appendix section simply includes copies of supporting documents regarding the content of your business plan that includes, but is not limited to: pictures of products, business registration papers, licensing and permit papers, trademark (or service mark) and patent papers, insurance policies, asset appraisals, partnership and employee contracts, market surveys, references, etc.

CHAPTER 7,

THE BASICS OF TAXES

CHAPTER 7

THE BASICS OF TAXES

Tax is a compulsory contribution to federal, state, and local revenue levied by the government on property, personal income, and business income. In the United States, income taxes are applied by rate according to tax brackets that specify volumes of annual income from small to large. As the volumes of annual income increase per bracket, the tax rate increases as well. Individuals, married couples filing jointly, and businesses are taxed annually according to their volume of annual income. Income is money received for work performed or through returns on investments. Income can be either earned, unearned, or a combination of both. Earned income is income such as salary, wages, commissions, or professional fees gained from the labor or services of an individual or business entity. Unearned income is income such as interest and dividend gains. Gross income is all the income (both earned and unearned) that an individual, married couple filing jointly, or business entity garners during a taxable year. A taxable year (also called tax year) is a calendar year or fiscal year used for annual accounting and tax computation. Income tax is tax levied on income. Net income is the balance of gross income that is left after the deduction of tax or other contributions from gross income. Taxable income is the total amount of income that is subject to taxation after all allowable exemptions, deductions, and credits have been applied to gross income for a given period.

The basics of filing and paying income taxes generally consist of reporting all income on designated forms known as returns or tax returns, paying due taxes on personal and/or business income, and applying a lawful system of exemptions, deductions, tax credits, and adjustments to gross income to get a refund (in whole or in part) on the taxes paid. A return (or tax return) is a designated form that is to be completed by individuals, couples filing jointly, and businesses to show taxable income, allowable deductions, exemptions, credits, and the computation of the tax due. Exemptions are amounts of income exempted from tax and deducted from the adjusted gross income as provided by law. Deductions (also called tax write-offs) are amounts of income that are allowed to be subtracted from the taxable income. Deductions can be either standard or itemized. Standard deductions are amounts of income that are set by tax law and allowed to be subtracted from adjusted gross income if the taxpayer does not itemize deductions. Itemized deductions are amounts that are set by tax law and allowed to be subtracted from adjusted gross income for specifically recorded items if the total of the deductions exceeds the standard deduction amount. Tax credits are amounts that can be subtracted from the gross income in the calculation of taxable income, but is distinguished from deductions and exemptions. Adjusted gross income is the gross income decreased by deductions. Tax refunds are refunds on taxes paid for a given period resulting from allowed tax exemptions, deductions, and credits.

Property tax is based on the assessed value of the property and is imposed on a local level. Property tax can vary from locality to locality, so be sure to check with your local assessors office and/or commissioner of revenue regarding more information on property tax in the particular locality in which you reside or have real estate located in or plan to have real estate located in. Real estate transfer tax (also called conveyance fee) is an amount imposed on the transfer of property (such as gift tax or estate tax), and is usually based on a rate per $1,000 dollars of the cost of the property or any part thereof.

There are also a wide range of other taxes that may apply to you in your business/commercial, investment, and/or real estate affairs— so be sure to do your research and/or consult with a tax advisor.

As an inmate you will have to have someone else (such as a power of attorney, trustee, authorized concierge service provider, etc.) take care of your tax preparation and filing.

CHAPTER 8,

ORGANIZING YOUR PAPERWORK

CHAPTER 8

ORGANIZING YOUR PAPERWORK

Being organized is key in the pursuit of business success. This is because as your business grows from the starting point, your loads of paperwork will gradually increase more and more over time, and if you fail to keep your paperwork organized, you could (and most likely will) suffer from confusion and lost documents resulting in a lack of follow-ups, missed opportunities, and financial turmoil— to list a few.

To avoid the headache and possibility of business failure, it is wise to develop a suitable filing system to organize and maintain your files in such a way that will allow you to locate necessary paperwork when needed in a timely manner.

A simple filing system generally consists of alphabetically and chronologically storing paperwork by category and subcategories, however, a more complex filing system may consist of numerically, alphabetically, and chronologically storing paperwork by category and subcategories. For example, with a simple filing system you can start off with six category file folders for record keeping: (1) financial records folder; (2) contractual records folder; (3) records of contacts and correspondence folder; (4) records of licensing and permits folder; (5) records of business plans, start-up information, notes and property folder; and (6) records of inventory folder. As you begin to store paperwork, file it alphabetically and chronologically in each file folder by category. As each file folder category begins to expand where it can be divided into subcategories, use dividers (such as a simple plain sheet of paper labeled with the individual subcategory per subcategory) to divide the subcategories for better file navigation. As each file folder category begins to expand requiring the need for additional file folders, use additional file folder per category as needed and number them chronologically.

It is also wise to create, update, and maintain a table of contents for your filing system that lists the individual categories and subcategories with file folder references for even better file navigation.

Keep in mind that the load of paperwork you are allowed to keep as an inmate may be limited according to your facility rules and regulations governing offender property. Therefore, you may need to have your files stored elsewhere in the event that your paperwork expands a bit too far. You may want to consider taking advantage of technology and have your family, spouse, power of attorney, trustee, or chosen concierge service provider to scan, store and maintain a copy of all your files on a flash drive to minimize the need of physical space, while allowing your files to be accessible on demand. This also allows you to protect yourself by having a back-up copy of all your records. Also, it's wise to maintain a copy of your files at two or more different locations to be on the safe side.

CHAPTER 9,

GETTING THE BALL ROLLING

CHAPTER 9

GETTING THE BALL ROLLING

First things first, you have to consider what you want to do, how you want to do it, and how much it will cost you to do it. This process usually requires research for accuracy, and lots of planning. Regardless of whatever it is that you want to do, you need to have a well thought-out plan. This includes deciding how you will operate and whether you want to operate under a registered business structure or just want to engage in commercial activity as an opportunistic entrepreneur without a registered business structure. Doing business under a registered business structure has its benefits and makes an overall statement of professionalism, yet may not be for everyone. Some people are better at (and would be better off) just wheeling and dealing. Wheeling and dealing or doing business via business deals has its benefits as well, yet these benefits are more centered around leisure, low start-up and overhead costs, and flexibility.

For inmates, operating online is the best and most convenient option. Operating online allows maximum exposure via the world wide web at a relatively low cost, yet costs may vary depending on the services you use (i.e. for a domain name, hosting, web design, online promotion, etc.)

With the use of one or more key tools of convenience it is extremely convenient to set-up and operate online and/or over the phone. The primary key tools of convenience are prisoner concierge services, email forwarding services, local phone number providers, web design services, web hosting services, crowdfunding, online social media outlets, pen pal connection services, installment purchase plans, selling on consignment, fulfillment services, and storage box services.

Prisoner concierge services are general service providers that specialize in working with incarcerated individuals collectively. Their services often range from simple internet information searches to advanced prisoner banking services and more. Most prisoner concierge services allow special requests for services, however, they warn against requesting services that will violate your institution's rules, and they will not provide any illegal services.

Email forwarding services are companies that forward emails to and from inmates to third parties. Emails to be forwarded are usually processed several times a week, yet can vary as to how many emails or times emails can be forwarded on a weekly basis depending on the email forwarding service provider.

Email forwarding services are extremely relevant and necessary due to the fact that the majority of companies, and people alike, now use emails instead of the traditional snail mail to avoid and/or eliminate the cost of postage, paper, and envelopes. Some companies, and people alike, don't even provide a mailing address anymore, they just provide a web address, phone number, fax number, and an email address— this makes it very difficult for inmates to contact them for business. Fortunately, email forwarding services allow inmates to forward and receive emails for business and/or personal purposes.

Local phone number providers offer local numbers for just about anywhere in the world to help inmates save money by converting long distance calls to your family, friends, or business associates into local calls. Local phone numbers are connected to the phone number of your distant family member, friend, or business associate so that the calls from you to them pass through as local calls.

Web design services produce web sites from the ground up for clients. Upon completion of the website and after full payment for service, web designers transfer all rights to the newly created websites over to the clients so that they may proceed to upload them to the world wide web via a web hosting service and register their newly created web sites with one or more search engines (among other things).

Web hosting services host your website, usually for a reasonable monthly fee, and allows your website to be accessed online via the worldwide web. Some popular web hosting services include web.com, godaddy.com, and wix.com.

Crowdfunding represents particular crowds of people willing to help fund you or a cause. Crowdfunding sites are online fundraising mediums that allow people to obtain funding from others online. These sites allow you to introduce your business or project and your financial needs, and ask the people/crowd to help fund you. Funds are usually deposited directly from the individual donors into the account set up for you with the crowdfunding site, and are allocated to you on a later date after a deduction for service fees and donation fees. To locate sites that specialize in crowdfunding, you can google the term "crowdfunding" or "crowdfunding sites."

Online social media outlets are websites like Facebook, Linkedin, Myspace and mocospace that allow you to create a profiles and connect with people all over the world.

Pen pal connection services are companies that seek to connect incarcerated individuals with people in the free world. They allow inmates to either place an ad on their website to be seen by potential pen friend, or to get a listing of pen friends who have made their contact information available for inmates to contact them. While some pen pal connection services are free, others usually charge a service fee.

Installment purchase plans (also called installment plans) allow you to make purchases of products or services and make use of the products or services while you are paying for them.

Selling on consignment generally consists of suppliers giving merchants goods up-front and allowing the merchants to pay down the cost of goods as the goods are sold. Usually a percentage of each unit sold over a 30 day period is added up and paid to the supplier monthly in monthly intervals until the goods are paid in full. The merchant is also responsible for any goods lost, stolen, or damaged while in his or her care. However, consignment terms may vary from supplier to supplier.

Fulfillment services are companies that charge you a monthly fee to hold your inventory in their storage facility and fill the orders placed by your customers by picking, packing, and shipping the specified orders to your customers as though it came directly from you or your business. With fulfillment services you can push to become one of the largest retailers in the world without ever having to touch the actual inventory that you sell.

Storage box services provide storage box space that may vary depending on the storage box service. Storage boxes are necessary for many reasons. They allow inmates to store away important information/documents for safekeeping.

Now that you are familiar with the key tools of convenience, let's follow a few basic steps to get the creative juices flowing.

Step One. Get the contact information to several individual prisoner concierge services, email forwarding services, local phone number providers, etc., and contact them for their service brochure with pricing. See what services are available at what prices, then do a service and price comparison to determine which ones best suit your needs and price budget. Keep in mind to always record the response turnaround time of service providers. Even if a service provider has the best services and/or prices, what good is it if they always respond to you months after your inquiry or service request. Always remember that fast turnaround is key.

Step Two. Once you have received and reviewed the information from the service providers, review your facility's operational procedures governing "inmate correspondence" and "inmate finances" to maintain compliance in all your affairs. This information should be available to you through your facility's library and/or law library.

Step Three. Take the necessary steps to open up an email forwarding account with an email forwarding service, or have an email account set up and managed by family or friends. This will put you in a position to reach businesses and their key personnel with your business proposal(s) via email and allow you to be reached via email by potential business prospects as well. Note: Some facilities have inmate correspondence policies that prohibit inmates from receiving print-outs of their email in the mail from email forwarding services, but they allow inmates to receive print-outs of email in the mail from family and friends as general correspondence mail. If the facility that you are housed in has this policy, contact the email forwarding service and inform them of this, then ask them if the two of you can make arrangements that will allow you to receive your emails and still comply with said policy. If they are unwilling to do so, you can still set up the email forwarding account and use it just for sending out emails in which you can inform the recipient to contact you at your physical mailing address (or other) due to your limited to no internet access.

Due to state and federal D.O.C.'s contracting with JPay, more and more facilities are allowing inmates to send and receive emails via a facility kiosk machine. Inmates can only email people who are on their contact list. For someone in the free world to get on an inmates contact list, they must initiate contact by either going to JPay.com or accessing the JPay mobile app, open up an account and send an email to the inmate or inmates to establish their names on that inmate's or those inmates' contact list so that inmate or those inmates can exchange emails with them whenever. If your state or federal facility is under contract with JPay and allows emails via the facility's kiosk machine, it is your responsibility to get the word out and have both people and companies alike to get on your contact list so you can exchange emails with them directly. If your facility is or is not under contract with JPay and does not allow emails via a facility kiosk machine, just know that that's why email forwarding services exist.

Step Four. Consider setting up local phone numbers to that you will be able to call your power of attorney, trustee, family, and/or friends regarding assistance with your affairs.

Step Five. Use the prisoner concierge services to do research on what you need researched or have your family and/or friends assist you with online research on the things you need researched. Once you have your facts right, start putting together your plan according to the facts backed by research.

Step Six. If you will be needing funds, have a prisoner concierge service, your family, or your friends help you set up a crowdfunding account and launch a fundraising campaign in efforts to get a little (or a lot) of financial assistance.

Step Seven. Assuming that you already have your plans together, it's time to contact potential power of attorneys and/or trustee to negotiate terms of contract (i.e., duties, duration of contract, compensation for general labor, etc.) in efforts to secure one or more power of attorneys and/or trustees. Understand that a power of attorney and/or trustee can be either a family member, friend, or other pre-paid or commissioned personnel.

It's best to have a detailed business plan for the power of attorney or trustee to follow as a guidance tool in carrying out your wishes— just be sure to establish a "confidentiality agreement," and if necessary, a "do not compete agreement" with anyone you plan to discuss your plans with. Furthermore, you can give your power of attorney and/or trustee a detailed instructional to-do list pre-weekly, pre-monthly, or via email, phone, and/or snail mail to better coordinate your business affairs.

Once an inmate and the potential power of attorney and/or trustee have reached an agreement and have established the date that service is to begin, on that date service can begin.

Keep in mind that although a power of attorney and/or a trustee can be necessary for you to maximize your ability to execute and otherwise manage your entrepreneurial affairs, some business deals can be made by you without the need of a power or attorney or trustee.

Step Eight. It is essential to create an online presence by launching either a website, social media page (i.e., Facebook page, etc.), pen pal connection page, or a combination of the three. Your presence online can make the difference necessary for you to reach success, so get creative and take full advantage of websites, social media pages, and pen pal connection pages. Also, take advantage of search engine optimization services and social media marketing services in efforts to create buzz and be found online.

Step Nine. Strongly consider using storage boxes because storage box space can be used to store a copy of all your important documents for safekeeping. Anything can go wrong at the facility that you are housed in, so to protect yourself against the possibility of lost, stolen, or damaged business documents, try to keep a spare copy of everything stored in one or more secondary locations (e.g., have a copy of all your important documents on one or more flash drives and then have them stored in one or more different storage box locations).

Depending on your plans you can factor in the other available tools of convenience to assist you in your path to entrepreneurial progress. Be creative. How you utilize these tools of convenience and general services is ultimately up to you.

CHAPTER 10,

MAKING DEALS

CHAPTER 10

MAKING DEALS

Making deals is the heart of business, so if you are or can become very skilled and prolific with business deal making, your chances of success are high. Making deals generally consist of an offer, some negotiating, and arriving at an agreement. This is the "offer and acceptance" element as discussed in Chapter 2.

If you want to make business deals you have to reach out in such a way to connect with potential business associates by means of contacting potential business associates and making yourself accessible so that you can be contacted by potential business associates.

Understand that everything starts with an idea. For example: Let's say that you come up with something that you believe will be a good business venture or simply good for business, yet it will require a collaboration of you and another business for it to go anywhere near as planned. You will have to make and submit a business proposal (offer) to that business that highlights your idea or ideas, how they stand to mutually gain/benefit from said idea or ideas, and any suggested terms of agreement.

A business proposal (offer) can be in the form of a letter, email, or verbal communication, and can be either simple or complexed. Here we will go over the basic structure of a simple business proposal to better help you grasp its concept.

The basic structure of a business proposal consists of several paragraphs containing brief and clear-cut information geared to gain overall acceptance. This information includes:

- Who you are
- Who the recipient or recipients are (and their contact information if the business proposal is in written form)
- Your contact information (clear and complete)
- The business that you are representing (if any)
- A brief summary regarding your idea or ideas (if you want to put some protection on the disclosure of your idea or ideas to a recipient or recipients, you can require a confidentiality agreement regarding your idea or ideas prior to a full disclosure of your idea or ideas with said recipient or recipients. keep this in mind when you are drafting this portion of your business proposal)
- A brief summary regarding the project or task that you are proposing (tell the recipient or recipients what you're trying to do as far as collaborating with them)
- A clear explanation regarding the possible benefit or benefits of this deal (tell the recipient or recipients how they stand to gain/benefit from the proposed deal)
- Third-party references regarding the business proposal (if any)

In closing, always invite the recipient or recipients of your business proposal to take action.

Figure 10.1 -gives an example of a simple business proposal letter.

Figure 10.1.

Travis E. Williams
Productions
1234 Williams Lane, #38
Progress, VA 76969
Phone: 804-000-0000
Email: tewpro@www

Inmates for Entrepreneurial Progress
4321 Progress Blvd.
Virginia, VA 71169
August 29, 2015

Re: "Business proposal".

Dear Inmates for Entrepreneurial Progress,

Hi. My name is Travis E. Williams, of Travis E. Williams Productions. l am the founder and CEO, and l am contacting you today regarding a co-marketing opportunity that l believe will be beneficial for both "Inmates for Entrepreneurial Progress" and "Travis E. Williams Productions".

As you may know, "Travis E. Williams Productions" creates educational materials geared towards providing inmates (and the family and loved ones of inmates) with the need to know information necessary for inmates to legally pursue entrepreneurial success while they are still incarcerated.

I am aware of Inmates for Entrepreneurial Progress and it's mission, and therefore figured that a co-marketing arrangement would be mutually beneficial.

l am currently planning to launch a marketing campaign by November 1st of this year and l would really like you to be a part of this campaign.

If this is something that you wish to entertain, and or for more information, please contact me no later than September 29th.

Thank you for your time.

Sincerely

Travis E. Williams

CHAPTER 11,

INVESTING

CHAPTER 11

INVESTING

For starters, let's define the word invest. To invest means to put money to use (through purchase or expenditure) in something that offers potential profitable returns such as interest or income or increased value.

While there are a massive variety of investment options available, you must know and understand that every investment involves some degree of risk whether it be low, moderate, high, or anywhere in between. It is up to you to know your risk tolerance and to do your research on the investment options available that best suit you and your investment goals. Financial advisors and brokers can assist you along the way whenever or if every you need assistance with your investment goals. The Financial Planning Association (FPA), can assist you with linking up with financial advisors and more. Their full contact information is provided in the resource section of this guide. Just be sure to do your research on the person's or firm's professional history and legitimacy (i.e., are they licensed?). To find licensing, employment, and disciplinary information, you can contact or have someone else contact the Financial Industry Regulatory Authority (FINRA). Their full contact information is provided in the resource section of this guide.

Some of the basic types of investment options are Certificate of deposits (CD's), Bonds and Bond Funds, Index Funds, Money Market Funds, Mutual Funds, Roth IRA's, Stocks, and Traditional IRA's — among other available investment options.

- A certificate of deposit(CD) is a written acknowledgment issued by a bank, verifying that it has received a specified sum of money from a named person or entity for a fixed term with a specified interest rate.
- Bonds and Bond Funds. These are known as fixed-income securities due to the fact that the income they pay is fixed when the bond is sold to you. We covered bonds in Chapter 5 under "stock corporations". Bonds and bond funds usually invest in corporate and government dept obligations.
- Index funds. An index fund is a fund, such as a mutual fund or pension fund, with a portfolio that consists of many of the securities listed in a

major stock index in efforts to match the performance of the stock market.

- Money market funds. A money market fund is a mutual fund that invests in the money market, usually in the form of short-term bonds. On average they pay more than a savings account but not as much as a CD(certificate of deposit).

- Mutual funds. A mutual fund is an investment company that functions by issuing shares continuously with an obligation to repurchase them from the shareholders on demand. They invest in a variety of securities such as stocks, bonds, and money market securities.

- Roth IRA's. Roth IRA's are personal savings plans that allow earnings that remain in the account to go untaxed.

- Stocks. Stocks were covered in Chapter 5 of this guide under stock corporations.

- Traditional IRA's. Traditional IRA's are personal savings plans that provides tax advantages for retirement savings.

Some questions to ask yourself is:

- How much should you invest?
- What is the investment term (i.e., how long will you have to wait until your investment matures)?
- How often should you invest?
- How quick can you get your money back from your investment?
- What will you earn on your investment?
- How much risk is involved in the investment?
- What options are available to diversify your investments?
- Are there any available tax advantages to the investments at hand?

Although we have discussed some of the basic investment options available, the scope of investing is a vast subject with vast methods. Take the time to contact a financial advisor regarding your financial planning. This will prove to be one of the best decisions made in addition to obtaining and reading this book.

CHAPTER 12,

ENGAGING IN REAL ESTATE

CHAPTER 12

ENGAGING IN REAL ESTATE

Engaging in real estate involves the acquisition, management, and sale or lease of real property, and consists of deeds, contracts and other agreements, and taxes for the most part.

The process of acquiring real estate generally consist of making an offer to purchase the real estate at hand. At this point, there is usually some price negotiations, and if an agreement is met, the terms of agreement are set forth in a written contractual agreement. Money is then paid to the seller in exchange for the deed to the real estate at hand and the buyer and the seller both sign the written contractual agreement acknowledging the terms of agreement. At this time the buyer is responsible for registering the newly purchased real estate with the local city or county's office for proof of title transfer and ownership. At this stage, the city or county's office may require you to pay a transfer tax and or other registration fee's. Depending on the State that the real estate is located in, property taxes may be required.

As for financing the real estate purchase, there are several ways to go but here we will highlight the top three. You could finance the whole purchase on your own with 100% of your own money. You can obtain financing from a bank or other financial lender and be subject to a mortgage and making mortgage payments. Or you can purchase the real estate through owner financing. Of these ways to finance the purchase of real estate, the best and most flexible way is owner financing. Owner financing usually provides the best APR rates and payment plans (not to mention the fact that owners can and most likely will be more forgiving regarding late payments and other unforeseen financial road blocks you may encounter along the way).

For those of you who are looking to make a healthy profit buying and selling real estate with little to no money down, "real estate options" are your best bet. With a real estate option you have control of the real estate at hand without having to buy it first. This option grants you the exclusive right to purchase the real estate or not, or sell that property or the option itself to someone else. During the duration of the option, the owner holds title of the property and is responsible for all costs associated with the property such as taxes and maintenance. However, you have the exclusive right to buy the property or not. During the term of your option, no one else can buy or sell the particular real estate at hand. If the owner sells the particular real estate at hand to someone else during the term of the option, you may be entitled to the money the owner receives over the amount you agreed to purchase the property for. Also, if the owner sells the real estate for less than what he or she agreed to sell the property to you for in the option, you may be entitled to receive the difference from the owner/seller.

Let's say you find a privately owned piece of property that's priced at $ 25,000 dollars and you want to option it because you see potential to make a profit of about $3,000 to $ 5,000 dollars. What you would do is contact the owner of the real estate and make an offer. You say, "Hi. I am very interested in purchasing the real estate that you are selling for $ 25,000 dollars. Would you be willing to enter into an agreement granting me the option to purchase the real estate within an agreed upon term with or without a minimum down payment?". If the owner agrees, you proceed to signing the option agreement. Once the option agreement is signed, the clock is ticking for you to make a move and get that property or the option itself sold in efforts to turn a profit. If you or the person you assign the option to does not purchase the property by the option exercise date, the exclusive right under the option terminates and all rights are forwarded back to the owner of the property.

Assignment clauses allow you to assign the option obligation to someone else during the term of the option. Any time the you assign your option obligations to someone else, it is your responsibility to give the owner proper notice.

A sample option agreement, assignment agreement, and notice of assignment letter is provided in the appendix section of this guide. Remember to take your time, plan carefully, and don't be afraid to ask for help if and when you need it.

APPENDIX A,

POWER OF ATTORNEY QUESTIONNAIRE

APPENDIX A

POWER OF ATTORNEY QUESTIONNAIRE

GENERAL INFORMATION
Full name: _____
Mailing address: _____
_____
_____

Home phone: _____
Cell phone: _____
Work phone: _____
Email address: _____

Gender: Male [] Female[] Other[]
Date of birth: _____
Social security number: _____
Marital status: Single [] Married [] Divorced [] Widowed [] Other []

Name of emergency contact: _____
Address: _____
_____
_____

Phone number: _____
Cell phone: _____
Work phone: _____
Email address: _____

What exactly do you need a power of attorney for?:
_____

_____

How many "attorney-in-fact's" do you want/need?: _____

If you're planning to have more than one attorney-in-fact, are they to act by unanimous agreement, by majority agreement, independently, or do you want them to alternate?: _____

List the full name and all contact information for each designated attorney-in-fact:

1.) Attorney-in-fact name: _____
Address: _____
_____
_____

Phone#: _____
Cell#: _____
Work#: _____
Email address: _____

2.) Attorney-in-fact name: _____
Address: _____
_____
_____

Phone#: _____
Cell#: _____
Work#: _____
Email address: _____

3.) Attorney-in-fact name: _____
Address: _____
_____
_____

Phone#: _____
Cell#: _____
Work#: _____
Email address: _____

4.) Attorney-in-fact name: _____
Address: _____
_____
_____

Phone#: _____
Cell#: _____
Work#: _____
Email address: _____

5.) Attorney-in-fact name: _____
Address: _____
_____
_____

Phone#: _____
Cell#: _____
Work#: _____
Email address: _____

6.) Attorney-in-fact name: _____
Address: _____
_____
_____

Phone#: _____

Cell#: _____
Work#: _____
Email address: _____

If you want them to alternate, list the order that you want them to alternate:

_____
_____

POWER OF YOUR ATTORNEY(S)-IN-FACT

Do you want to grant "limited" or "general" power of attorney?:_____

What matters do you want to grant your attorney(s)-in-fact the power to act in and on your behalf in?:

[] Banking and all other financial transactions
[] Business affairs
[] Investment affairs
[] Real estate affairs, [] but may not sell my property without my approval
[] Tangible personal property
[] Retirement plans
[] Taxes
[] All other as may be designated by myself

Shall your attorneys-in-fact make reports?: _____ If so, how often shall reports be submitted and to whom shall the reports be submitted?:
_____

Will your attorneys-in-fact receive compensation for acting on your behalf?: _____ If so, in what form will they be receiving compensation?:
_____

APPENDIX B,

LIMITED POWER OF ATTORNEY

APPENDIX B

LIMITED POWER OF ATTORNEY

I, _____(inmate name), as principal, do hereby appoint _____(name of agent), and grant limited power of attorney to the same, to act on and or sign in my behalf in any and all matters and circumstances herein specified and described below:

_____
_____
_____

_____(list everything that the agent is to have power to do on your behalf here).

Both parties (principal and agent) acknowledge and agree that the attorney-in-fact/authorized agent herein is not acting, and shall not be deemed to be acting as an accommodation party for the principal, and his or her acts and actions do not comprise an accommodation, nor an acceptance of liability.

In the original jurisdiction of the State of _____ (name of state), this power of attorney is signed on this _____(day) day of _____(month) _____(year), and to become effective immediately and shall remain in effect until this power of attorney is fulfilled or has been revoked, suspended or terminated in writing by principal written notice to the designated attorney-in-fact.

Principal: _____ (inmate signature).

Attorney-in-fact: _____ (agent signature).

State of _____ (name of state).

City/County of _____

Sworn to, and subscribed before me, in my presence on this _____ day of _____.

_____
Notary Public

My commission expires: _____

APPENDIX C,

GENERAL POWER OF ATTORNEY

APPENDIX C

GENERAL POWER OF ATTORNEY

I, _____ (name of inmate), as principal, do hereby appoint _____ (name of agent), and grant general power of attorney to the same, to act on and or sign in my behalf in any and all matters and circumstances herein specified and described below:

1.) Open, maintain or close bank accounts, brokerage accounts, and similar accounts with other financial institutions, as may be designated by myself.

2.) Sell, exchange, buy, invest, or reinvest assets or property owned by me.

3.) Enter into binding agreements/contracts on my behalf.

4.) Sell, lease, convey, manage, mortgage, repair, improve, or perform acts regarding any of my property now owned or later acquired.

5.) And to do any other act as though I myself am doing it, as may be designated by myself.

Both parties (principal and agent) acknowledge and agree that the attorney-in-fact/authorized agent herein is not acting, and shall not be deemed to be acting as an accommodation party for the principal, and his or her acts and actions do not comprise an accommodation, nor an acceptance of liability.

In the original jurisdiction of the State of _____ (name of state), this power of attorney is signed on this _____ (day) day of _____ (month) _____ (year), and to become effective immediately and shall remain in effect until this power of attorney is fulfilled or has been revoked, suspended or terminated in writing by principal written notice to the designated attorney-in-fact.

Principal: _____ (inmate signature).

Attorney-in-fact: _____ (agent signature).

State of _____ (name of state).

City/County of _____

Sworn to, and subscribed before me, in my presence on this _____ day of _____.

_____
Notary Public

My commission expires: _____

APPENDIX D,

AGENT'S CERTIFICATION AS TO THE VALIDITY OF POWER OF ATTORNEY AND AGENT'S AUTHORITY

APPENDIX D

AGENT'S CERTIFICATION AS TO THE VALIDITY OF POWER OF ATTORNEY AND AGENT'S AUTHORITY

State of _____ (state name)

City/County of _____ (name of city or county)

I, _____ (name of agent), certify under penalty of perjury that _____ (name of principal) granted me authority as an attorney-in-fact or successor attorney-in-fact in a power of attorney dated _____ (list the date of the actual power of attorney).

I further certify that to my knowledge:

1.) The principal is alive and has not revoked the power of attorney or my authority to act under the power of attorney and the power of attorney and my authority to act under the power of attorney have not been terminated;

2.) If the power of attorney was drafted to become effective upon the happening of an event or contingency, the event or contingency has occurred; and

3.) If I was named as a successor attorney-in-fact, the prior attorney-in-fact is no longer able or willing to serve.

SIGNATURE AND ACKNOWLEDGMENT

_____ (agents signature) _____ (date).
_____ (agents name in print)

Agents address: _____

_____
_____

Agents phone #: _____

Agents cell #: _____

Agents email address: _____

State of _____ (name of state).

City/County of _____

Sworn to, and subscribed before me, in my presence on this ____ day of _____.

_____
Notary Public

My commission expires: _____

APPENDIX E,

SAMPLE TRUST AGREEMENT

APPENDIX E

SAMPLE TRUST AGREEMENT

This Trust Agreement replaces and supersedes all previous Trust Agreements, if any, and is made between _____ (print name of trustor/inmate here), Trustor, who is currently incarcerated in the State of _____ (State name here), and _____ (print name of trustee here), Trustee, of _____ (full address of trustee here). The above named Trustor shall hereinafter be called "Trustor", and the above named Trustee shall hereinafter be called "Trustee".

    1.) Transfer in Trust

Trustor hereby assigns, transfers, and otherwise conveys to Trustee the sum of $ _____ (amount of money placed in the trust here) and the following property: _____

_____

_____

_____ (list each item of property, to include addresses and any other property identifiers, here). Receipt of said sum and property is acknowledged by Trustee. The described sum and property, and all additions made thereto, shall be held in trust by the Trustee for the uses, purposes, terms, and conditions set forth in this Trust Agreement. The Trustee hereby accepts assignments and overall transfers made to Trustee for the benefit of the Trustor (and or any named beneficiaries).

2.)   Additions made to Trust Estate

The Trustor and any other person or entity shall have the right to make monetary and in-kind contributions to this trust. When such contributions are made and received by the Trustee it shall become part of this trust.

3.)   Identification of Beneficiary

The above named Trustor shall be the only beneficiary of this Trust Agreement. The Trustee shall hold the Trust Estate for the Trustor and the trust shall bear the name of the Trustor.

4.)   Terminations and Distributions

    i. This trust shall terminate upon the death of the Trustor or when the Trustor is released from incarceration. Upon termination he Trustee shall transfer all funds and property assigned to the Trustee under this trust agreement.

ii. For the duration of this trust agreement, the Trustee may distribute portions of net income and principal to the Trustor as may be reasonably necessary to provide for the support, and overall welfare of the Trustor.

5.) Trustee Power

The Trustee shall have the power to act on the Trustors behalf in light of this trust agreement as though the Trustor would act upon proper notice to Trustor and any Attorneys-in-fact assigned by the Trustor regarding major decisions such as the sell, purchase, or other acquisition of property, and any allocation of funds outside of what's necessary to maintain the matters of this trust.

6.) Compensation

The Trustee shall be entitled to _____ (list the compensation and when it's allowed here) for the Trustees services rendered under this trust agreement.

7.) Successors

The Trustor shall appoint a successor Trustee in the event that the acting Trustee can or will no longer act as Trustee.

8.) Governing Law

This trust agreement shall be governed by the laws of _____(list the state name here).

WHEREFORE, the Trustor and Trustee enters into this trust agreement on this _____ (day here) day of _____ (month and year here).

Signature of Trustor: _____

Signature of Trustee: _____

State of _____ (name of state here)

In the City/County of _____(name of City/County here)

Sworn to and subscribed before me on this _____ (day here) day of _____(month and year here).
_____

Notary Public

My commission expires: _____

APPENDIX F,

(SAMPLE) CERTIFICATE/MEMORANDUM OF TRUST AGREEMENT

APPENDIX F

(SAMPLE) CERTIFICATE/MEMORANDUM OF TRUST AGREEMENT

I, _____ (name of trustee), the undersigned Trustee, being first duly sworn, certifies that a Trust exists and states:

1.) The name/title of the Trust is: _____ (put the name of the trust here).

2.) The date of the Trust is: _____ (put the date of the trust here).

3.) The Trust tax identification number is: _____ (put the trust tax identification number here).

4.) The name and address of the current trustee acting on behalf of the above Trust is:

Name: _____

Address: _____
_____
_____

5.) The trustee shall have the power/authority to act on my behalf in any and all matters related to the above named Trust in good faith.

6.) The trust agreement and any amendment thereto is to be governed by the laws of _____ (put the name of the state here).

7.) The trust agreement related to this certificate/memorandum and any amendment thereto is still in full force and effect.

8.) This certificate/memorandum of Trust certifies the current status of the trust agreement.

Signature: _____ (trustee's signature)

Name: _____ (trustee's name in print)

State of _____ (name of state here)

City/County of _____ (city/county name here)

Sworn and subscribed to before me this _____(day) day of _____ (month and year).

_____

Notary Public

My commission expires: _____

APPENDIX G,

(SAMPLE) APPOINTMENT OF SUCCESSOR TRUSTEE

APPENDIX G

(SAMPLE) APPOINTMENT OF SUCCESSOR TRUSTEE

I, _____ (name of trustor here), hereby declare and certify that I am the trustor under the trust agreement dated _____ (date of trust agreement here), in trust and benefit of _____ (put the name or names of the beneficiaries here), as specified in the trust agreement. Under said trust agreement I reserved the right/power to name and otherwise appoint the succeeding trustees in the event of death, resignation, or inability to serve of the acting trustee.

In the event of death, resignation, or inability to serve, I hereby name and designate _____ (put the name of the successor trustee here), as trustee to succeed in said trust agreement.

The name, address, and contact information of the successor trustee is:

Name: _____

Address: _____
_____
_____

Phone #: _____

Cell #: _____

Email address: _____

Signature of Trustor: _____

Name of Trustor: _____ (in print)

State of _____ (name of state here)

City/County of _____ (city/county name here)

Sworn and subscribed to before me this _____ (day) day of _____ (month and year).

_____
Notary Public

My commission expires: _____

APPENDIX H,

CONFIDENTIALITY AGREEMENT

APPENDIX H

CONFIDENTIALITY AGREEMENT

I, the undersigned, as a duly authorized representative of _____(list the company, organization, or person here), in consideration for the disclosure of information/details relating to the _____ (list whether it's a idea, business proposal device, or other here) for _____(list it's purpose here), conceived or invented by, or otherwise assigned or licensed to _____(inmate name here), agree to keep all such information/details disclosed to me and all other company personnel for evaluation confidential:

1.) Unless written permission is granted by _____(inmate name here) or his/her authorized representative;

2.) Or until the expiration of seven (7) years from the signing date of this confidentiality agreement.

I understand that the disclosure of such information/details shall not be construed as granting a license, any right to ownership, or the likes. I further understand that this confidentiality agreement reflects the understanding between the parties mentioned herein this confidentiality agreement, and that this confidentiality agreement stands to safeguard all information/details disclosed for evaluation.

This confidentiality agreement supersedes all prior related discussions, understandings, and or agreements between the parties mentioned herein this confidentiality agreement.

Name: _____ (their name printed here)

Signature: _____ (their signature here)

Company name: _____ (company name here)

Inventor/Conceiver/Owner: _____ (inmate name here)

Sworn and subscribed to before me this _____ (day here) day of _____ (month and year here).

_____
Notary Public

My commission expires: _____

APPENDIX I,

OPTION AGREEMENT FOR THE PURCHASE OF REAL PROPERTY

APPENDIX I

OPTION AGREEMENT FOR THE PURCHASE OF REAL PROPERTY

This OPTION AGREEMENT, hereinafter referred to as "Agreement", is made and entered this ____(day of the month here) day of _____ (month and year here), by and between _____ (the inmate's full name in print here as the purchaser), Purchaser, hereinafter referred to as "Purchaser", and _____ (the persons full name of which is selling the real property goes here in print), Seller, hereinafter referred to as "Seller".

- The Seller is the owner of the real property herein described being and situated in the City/County of _____ (name of city or county here), State of _____ (name of the state here), such property having the physical address of _____ (physical address of the property here) and said property being more accurately described as follows:

    [place the legal description of the real property here (i.e., the recorded lot, block, and track description with all attachments) as described in the public records]

- The Purchaser desires to secure an option to purchase the above mentioned real property upon the terms and provisions as set forth herein.

THEREFORE, for good consideration the receipt and sufficiency of which is hereby acknowledged by both parties hereto. The Seller and Purchaser hereby agrees as follows:

1.) Definitions. For the purpose of this Agreement, the following terms mean as follows:

    (i)   "Closing date" means the last day of the closing term selected by the Purchaser;

    (ii)   "Execution Date" means the day upon which this Agreement shall be executed;

    (iii)   "Option Fee" means the total sum of the down payment on the purchase (if any), plus all closing costs, payable as set forth herein;

(iv) "Option Term" means the duration of time commencing on the Execution Date and ending on or before _____ (the date that the option agreement term ends here);

(v) "Option Exercise Date" means the date within the option term during which the Purchaser must provide written notice to the Seller to exercise his/her option to purchase.

2.) Grant of option. For and in consideration of the Option Fee payable to the Seller as set forth herein, the Seller grants the Purchaser the exclusive right and option to purchase the real property described above under the terms of this Agreement.

3.) Payment of option fee. The Purchaser agrees to pay $ _____ (negotiate at least a $50 to $100 dollar down payment) to the Seller as a down payment on the total purchase price of the real property described above plus all closing costs at the Execution Date.

4.) Exercise of option. The Purchaser may exercise his/her exclusive right to purchase the real property described above at anytime during the term of the Option Term pursuant to the option by providing the Seller with proper notice. If in the event the Purchaser chooses not to exercise his/her exclusive right to purchase the real property as described above during the Option Term, the Seller shall be entitled to retain the down payment and this Agreement will therefore become null and void with neither party herein having further liability or obligation under this Agreement.

5.) Contract for sale and purchase of real property. If Purchaser exercises his/her exclusive right to purchase, the Seller agrees to sell the real property described above under the following terms:

(i) Purchase price. The purchase price of the real property described above is $ _____ (the sell price of the real property here); however, the down payment shall be credited to the purchase price and the Purchaser shall pay the Seller the sum of $ _____ at closing;

(ii) Closing Date. The closing date shall be on or any time before _____ (the date here);

(iii) Closing costs. The costs of closing shall be the Purchaser's responsibility.

(iv) Default by Purchaser. If Purchaser fails to proceed with the closing the Seller shall be entitled to retain the down payment as damages with no further recourse against the Purchaser;

(v) Default by Seller. If the Seller fails to close the sale the Purchaser shall be entitled to either sue for money damages or for specific performance of the real property purchase.

- This Agreement shall apply to and be binding upon the parties hereto and their heirs, successors, or assigns.

WHEREFORE, both Seller and Purchaser agrees as provided in this Agreement the day and year first above written.

Seller's signature: _____

Purchaser's signature: _____

Witness:

Sworn and subscribed to before me this ____ (day of the month here) day of _____ (month and year here).

_____

Notary Public

My commission expires: _____

APPENDIX J,

ASSIGNMENT AGREEMENT

APPENDIX J

ASSIGNMENT AGREEMENT

This ASSIGNMENT AGREEMENT is made this ____(day of the month here) day of _____(month and year here), by and between _____(the inmate's full name in print here as the assignor), Assignor, hereinafter referred to as "Assignor", and _____(the persons full name of which you are assigning the option to goes here in print), Assignee, hereinafter referred to as "Assignee", in consideration of the mutual covenants contained herein and other valuable consideration, the sufficiency of which is hereby acknowledged, to wit:

- The Assignor entered into a contractual option agreement for purchase of real property with _____(the owners full name here — as the real property owner), hereinafter referred to as "Option Agreement", on the ____ (day of the month here) day of _____(month and year here). See attachment A (attach a copy of the original option agreement as "Attachment A").

- The option agreement has an expiration date of _____ (date that the option agreement expires here).

- The Assignor hereby wishes to assign all of his/her rights and obligations under said "Option Agreement" to Assignee, and

- The Assignor hereby certifies that proper notice of this assignment will be given to the owner and grantor of the option agreement at the signing of this assignment agreement.

- The Assignor and Assignee agrees as follows:

1.) That the Assignor shall assign all rights, and delegate all obligations under said option agreement to Assignee.

2.) Assignee hereby accepts the assignment of all of Assignor's rights and obligations under said option agreement.

3.) That Assignee must contact the owner and grantor of the option agreement regarding the assignment agreement within 7 days of the date of the assignment agreement.

The contact information for the owner and grantor of the option agreement is as follows:

Name: _____

Address: _____
_____
_____

Phone #: _____
Cell #: _____
Email: _____

    WHEREFORE, both Assignor and Assignee agrees as provided in this assignment agreement the day and year first above written.

Assignor's signature: _____

Assignor's name (in print): _____

Assignee's signature: _____

Assignee's name (in print): _____

Witness:

Sworn and subscribed to before me this ____ (day of the month here) day of _____ (month and year here).

_____

Notary Public

My commission expires: _____

[notary seal here]

APPENDIX K,

NOTICE OF ASSIGNMENT

APPENDIX K

NOTICE OF ASSIGNMENT

Dear _____ (owners full name in print here),

You are hereby notified that I, _____ (inmate's full name here), of whom you entered into an option agreement with on _____ (date that the option agreement was entered into here), have assigned said option agreement to _____ (the full name of the Assignee here).

    The Assignee under terms of assignment must contact the owner and grantor of the option agreement regarding the assignment agreement within 7 days of the date of the assignment agreement.

The Assignee's contact information is as follows:

Name: _____

Address: _____
_____
_____

Phone #: _____
Cell #: _____
Email: _____

    I hereby certify that the above notice of assignment was sent to the owner and grantor of the option agreement on this ____ (day of the month here) day of _____ (month and year here).

Assignor's signature: _____

APPENDIX L,

START UP STEPS

APPENDIX L

START-UP STEPS

The following is the basics steps for starting your own business as either a sole proprietorship, partnership, limited partnership, limited liability company, corporation, or business trust. Always remember that if ever you need help, answers, or additional information, the Small Business Administration can steer you right.

- A "sole proprietorship". This is relatively easy to set up. The main factors involved here are:

1.) The first step is to link up with someone you trust to be your business agent. You will need this person to act on your behalf under "contract of agency". This will allow them to legally carry out your business affairs.

2.) The 2nd step is to determine if you want the business to have your name or some other name. If it will have your name then all you have to worry about is securing an agent to act on your behalf in all business matters, deciding your business location, and securing the proper business licensing and permits. If you want your business to be named something other then your name, you will have to file that name with the local Circuit Court as an assumed/fictitious name. Researching and registering a fictitious name for your business if in the event you choose to operate your business under a fictitious business name. For example, my name is Travis Eugene Williams, however, if I want the name of my business to be "Inmates for Entrepreneurial Progress", I will have to research that name to make sure it's available. If it is available, then I would register it as an "assumed/fictitious name" with my local Circuit Court. (You can contact your local Circuit Court and request an "assumed/fictitious name" form along with filing instructions and the filing fee's associated with the process and they will provide you with what you need).

3.) The 3rd step is to determine if you will be operating online only or if you will be operating out of a street location or both. If you will be operating online only, have your business agent contact the local zoning authority to obtain a "home business permit"(You will need to comply with the local zoning regulations though). If you will be operating out of street location, you will still need to make sure that you are in compliance with zoning regulations.

4.) The 4th step is to have your business agent secure a business license from the local Commissioner of Revenue.

5.) determine if you will be required to obtain a Federal Employer Identification Number (EIN). If so, you will need to file an application for an Employer Identification Number (EIN) with the IRS.

6.) determine if you will be responsible for unemployment tax.

Once you have secured your business agent, business name, a business location, and proper business licensing and permits, you can legally do business through your business agent. Note: Sole proprietorships are usually not required to register with the State Corporation Commission or Secretary of State.

- A "partnership".

1.) secure business agent.

2.) secure a "partnership agreement/partnership statement" with partner/partners and prepare an "operating agreement" to govern the business.

3.) secure business name.

4.) determine location.

5.) register with your State Corporation Commission or Secretary of State by filing a "Statement of Partnership Authority" with them.

6.) determine if you will be required to obtain a Federal Employer Identification Number (EIN). If so, you will need to file an application for an Employer Identification Number (EIN) with the IRS.

7.) secure proper business licensing and permits.

- A "limited partnership".

1.) secure business agent.

2.) complete a "limited partnership agreement" with partner/partners.

3.) secure business name.

4.) determine location.

5.) register with your State Corporation Commission or Secretary of State by filing a "certificate of limited partnership" with them.

6.) determine if you will be required to obtain a Federal Employer Identification Number (EIN). If so, you will need to file an application for an Employer Identification Number (EIN) with the IRS.

7.) secure proper business licensing and permits.

- A "limited liability company(LLC)".

1.) secure business agent.

2.) secure/prepare a "management agreement to govern the LLC.

3.) secure business name.

4.) determine location.

5.) register with your State Corporation Commission or Secretary of State by filing a "articles of organization" with them.

6.) determine if you will be required to obtain a Federal Employer Identification Number (EIN). If so, you will need to file an application for an Employer Identification Number (EIN) with the IRS.

7.) open business accounts with banks, etc....

8.) secure proper business licensing and permits.

- A "corporation".

1.) secure business agent.

2.) prepare bylaws to govern the corporation.

3.) secure business name.

4.) determine location.

5.) register with your State Corporation Commission or Secretary of State by filing an "articles of incorporation" with them.

6.) determine if you will be required to obtain a Federal Employer Identification Number (EIN). If so, you will need to file an application for an Employer Identification Number (EIN) with the IRS.

7.) open business accounts with banks, etc...

8.) secure proper business licensing and permits.

- A "business trust".

1.) secure business agent.

2.) complete a "business trust agreement".

3.) secure business name.

4.) determine location.

5.) register with your State Corporation Commission or Secretary of State by filing an "articles of trust" with them.

6.) determine if you will be required to obtain a Federal Employer Identification Number (EIN). If so, you will need to file an application for an Employer Identification Number (EIN) with the IRS.

7.) open business accounts with banks, etc...

8.) secure proper business licensing and permits.

Contact your local circuit Court to obtain the necessary form and filing instructions for "fictitious/assumed names".

Contact your local City or County Commissioner of Revenue for all information on obtaining your business license.

Contact your local Department of Planning and Community Development for information on obtaining your home business permit.

For additional information and assistance regarding the start-up process, contact the nearest Small Business Development Center (SBDC).

APPENDIX M,

RESOURCES

APPENDIX M

RESOURCES

The following list of resources is provided for your benefit. Please take the time to read over them all and contact them as needed.

- Small Business Administration (SBA)
  409 3rd St., SW, Suite 7600
  Washington, DC 20416
  Toll free: 1-800-827-5722(Information)
  Phone: 704-344-6640
  Email: answerdesk@sba.gov
  Web: www.sba.gov

The SBA helps Americans start, build and grow businesses. Through an extensive network of field offices and partnerships the SBA aids, counsels, assists, and protects the interests of small business concerns.

- The Education Publications Center (EDPUBS)
  P.O. Box 22207
  Alexandria, VA 22304
  Toll free: 1-877-433-7827 (in English & Spanish)
  Phone: 1-877-576-7734
  Email: edpubs@edpubs.ed.gov
  Web: www.edpubs.gov

This office helps consumers identify and order free publications and resources from the U.S. Department of Education.

- Office of Vocational and Adult Education (OVAE)
  400 Maryland Ave., SW
  Washington, DC 20202-7100
  Phone: 202-245-7700
  Email: ovae@ed.gov

OVAE administers and coordinates programs that are related to adult education and literacy, career and technical education, and community colleges.

- Jump Start Coalition for Personal Financial Literacy
  919 18th St., NW, Suite 300
  Washington, DC 20006
  Toll free: 1-888-453-3822
  Phone: 202-466-8604
  Email: info@jumpstartcoalition.org
  Web: www.jumpstart.org

- United States Patent and Trademark Office (USPTO)
  P.O. Box 1450
  Arlington, VA 22313-1450
  Toll free: 1-800-786-9199
  Phone: 571-272-9950
  Email: usptoinfo@uspto.gov
  Web: www.uspto.gov

The USPTO grants patents for intellectual property and trademarks for brand names and symbols, protecting the rights of inventors and designers.

> Bureau of the Public Debt
> Treasury Direct
> P.O. Box 7015
> Parkersburg, WV 26106-7015
> Toll free: 1-800-722-2678

This agency borrows money to make sure that the federal government continues to operate. You can contact them to purchase bonds or to check on the maturity of bonds you have already purchased.

- Financial Planning Association (FPA)
  4100 E. Mississippi Ave., Suite 400
  Denver, CO 80246-3053
  Toll free: 1-800-322-4237
  Email: fpa@fpanet.org

The FPA is a leadership and advocacy organization connecting those who provide services with the consumers they serve. This organization is a resource for the public to find educational resources and financial planners to deliver advice using an ethical, objective, client-centered process.

- Financial Industry Regulatory Authority (FINRA)
  Office of Dispute Resolution
  1736 K St., NW
  Washington, DC 20006
  Phone: 301-590-6500
  Toll free: 1-800-289-9999
  Web: www.finra.org

FINRA is the largest independent regulator for all securities firms doing business in the U.S. The organization operates the largest dispute resolution forum in the securities industry for disputes between investors and securities firms.

- Direct Marketing Association (DMA)
  Department of Corporate Responsibility
  1615 L St., NW, Suite 1100

Washington, DC 20036
Phone: 202-955-5030
Email: consumer@the-dma.org
Web: www.dmachoice.org

The DMA is the trade association for organizations involved in direct marketing via direct mail, catalogs, the internet, telemarketing, magazines, and newspaper and TV ads. DMA's consumer website offers consumers options (free of charge) to better manage their mail.

- Direct Selling Association (DSA)
  1667 K St., NW, Suite 1100
  Washington, DC 20006
  Phone: 202-452-8866
  Email: info@dsa.org
  Web: www.dsa.org

DSA is the trade association of firms that manufacture and distribute goods and services sold directly to consumers.

- Internal Revenue Service (IRS)
  Toll free: 1-800-829-1040(for individuals)
  Toll free: 1-800-829-4933(for businesses)
  TTY: 1-800-829-4059
  www.irs.gov

Free tax help is available from the Internal Revenue Service 24 hours a day, 7 days a week. Contact them about electronic filing options, the status of refunds, printable tax forms and instructions, and linking up with preparers who can electronically file tax returns. The IRS provides informative publications for taxpayers. Among these publications, the top few to consider are: Starting a business and keeping records(Pub. 583); Accounting periods and methods(Pub. 538); Corporations(Pub. 542); Exempt status for your organization (Pub. 557); Understanding your EIN(Pub. 1635); and How to deprecate property(Pub. 946) — to list a few.

ABOUT THE AUTHOR

The author, Travis Eugene Williams, was sentenced to 38 years in the Virginia Department of Corrections back in 2005.

In efforts to become a better man he committed to learning, studying matters of business and business management, strengthening his communication skills, and rehabilitating his self while encouraging other inmates to do the same. He is a strong minded visionary and an ambitious entrepreneurial opportunist.

He is currently working to produce other projects and educational/informative materials geared towards helping inmates in their pursuit of rehabilitation and fulfilling their entrepreneurial aspirations (in whole or in part) while they are incarcerated.

He is asking inmates and the loved ones of those who are incarcerated to help spread the word regarding the "Inmates for Entrepreneurial Progress" movement and its overall mission.

For you inmates who seek to be the embodiment of ambition and positive change while letting your creative and potentially promising entrepreneurial light shine for all to see; For you inmates who seek to be better providers for your families and loved ones; For you inmates who seek to show that you deserve another chance—This Incarcerated Entrepreneurs Guide provides you with much needed information in a simple, easy to follow format.

This guide provides the need-to-know basics for power of attorneys, trustees, contracts, property, the essentials of business, business structures, taxes, raising funds, safeguarding important documents, getting started, and much more.

Words of encouragement:

> "Share your knowledge,
> Make a difference.
> Be a positive force for Change.
> Remember, you create your own reality."
> Author unknown

$15.95

INMATES FOR ENTREPRENEURIAL PROGRESS

A Guide to Legally Starting a Business, Investing, Engaging in Real Estate, and Doing Business via Business Deals While Incarcerated in the United States

By Travis E. Williams

2015

Made in the USA
Monee, IL
06 May 2024